Step-by-Step Transformations

Turning Wool into Sweaters

Amy Hayes

Cavendish Square

New York

Published in 2016 by Cavendish Square Publishing, LLC
243 5th Avenue, Suite 136, New York, NY 10016

First Edition

Website: cavendishsq.com

This publication represents the opinions and views of the author based on his or her personal experience, knowledge, and research. The information in this book serves as a general guide only. The author and publisher have used their best efforts in preparing this book and disclaim liability rising directly or indirectly from the use and application of this book.

CPSIA Compliance Information: Batch #WS15CSQ

All websites were available and accurate when this book was sent to press.

Library of Congress Cataloging-in-Publication Data

Hayes, Amy.
Turning wool into sweaters / Amy Hayes.
pages cm. — (Step-by-step transformations)
Includes index.
ISBN 978-1-50260-455-2 (hardcover) ISBN 978-1-50260-454-5 (paperback) ISBN 978-1-50260-456-9 (ebook)
1. Sweaters—Juvenile literature. 2. Woolen and worsted spinning—Juvenile literature. 3. Yarn—Juvenile literature. 4. Knitting—Juvenile literature. I. Title.
TT825.H3976 2015
746'.0432—dc23

2015009757

Editorial Director: David McNamara
Copy Editor: Cynthia Roby
Art Director: Jeffrey Talbot
Designer: Alan Sliwinski
Senior Production Manager: Jennifer Ryder-Talbot
Production Editor: Renni Johnson
Photo Research by J8 Media

Photos by: francesco de marco/Shutterstock.com, cover; Dorling Kindersley/Getty Images, cover; © iStockphoto.com/HeikeKampe, 5; Dalibor Seveljevic/Shutterstock.com, 7; francesco de marco/Shutterstock.com, 9; Celiafoto/Shutterstock.com, 11; Portland Press Herald/Getty Images, 13; Portland Press Herald/Getty Images, 15; © iStockphoto.com/danix, 17; truembie/Shutterstock.com, 19; Laurence Mouton/PhotoAlto/Getty Images, 21.

Printed in the United States of America

Contents

Sweaters are made from wool.

5

Wool is sheep's hair.

First, a farmer **shears**
the sheep.

7

Next, the dirtiest parts of the wool are taken out.

9

After that the wool is **carded**, or brushed through combs.

11

Now the wool is in a long strand.

13

Next, the strand is put on a spinning wheel.

The wheel spins the wool.

15

The spun wool is called **yarn**.

16

17

Yarn is **knit** with needles.

Finally the sweater is done!

Wool sweaters are nice
and warm.

21

New Words

carded (KARD-ed) Combed and collected together.

knit (NIT) To make a piece of clothing from yarn using needles or a machine.

shears (SHEERZ) Cuts the hair off.

yarn (YARN) Long, thin pieces of spun wool.

Index

About the Author

Amy Hayes lives in the beautiful city of Buffalo, New York. She has written several books for children, including the Machines That Work and the Our Holidays series for Cavendish Square.

About

Bookworms help independent readers gain reading confidence through high-frequency words, simple sentences, and strong picture/text support. Each book explores a concept that helps children relate what they read to the world in which they live.